THE QUIET IN ME

THE QUIET IN ME
PATRICK LANE

Poems

With an introduction by Lorna Crozier

**HARBOUR
PUBLISHING**

1 2 3 4 5 — 26 25 24 23 22

Harbour Publishing Co. Ltd.
P.O. Box 219, Madeira Park, BC, VON 2HO
www.harbourpublishing.com

Cover images: koi by Quality Stock Arts/Shutterstock; moon by travellight/Shutterstock
Edited by Lorna Crozier
Cover design by Rhonda Ganz
Text design by Carleton Wilson
Printed and bound in Canada
Printed on 100% recycled paper

Supported by the Province of British Columbia

Harbour Publishing acknowledges the support of the Canada Council for the Arts, the Government of Canada, and the Province of British Columbia through the BC Arts Council.

Library and Archives Canada Cataloguing in Publication
Title: The quiet in me : poems / Patrick Lane ; with an introduction by Lorna Crozier.
Names: Lane, Patrick, author. | Crozier, Lorna, 1948- writer of introduction.
Identifiers: Canadiana (print) 20220151385 | Canadiana (ebook) 20220151393 |
    ISBN 9781550179811 (softcover) | ISBN 9781550179828 (EPUB)
Subjects: LCGFT: Poetry.
Classification: LCC PS8523.A53 Q54 2022 | DDC C811/.54—dc23

For Patrick Lane's children and grandchildren,
for his beloved students,
and for his life-long friend and poetry publisher, Howie White

*"Sometimes we live far from the world
Without thought, and wanting."*

CONTENTS

LAST WORDS

And as long as you haven't experienced
this: to die and so to grow,
you are only a troubled guest
on the dark earth.
—Goethe

Though Patrick Lane may have known in his long and beautiful bones
that to die is to grow, as Goethe would have us believe, he was at the same
time "a troubled guest" on the earth. In my forty years with him, I knew no
one who loved the creatures and flora of the world more than he did, nor
anyone who was more distressed by the damage human beings perpetrate
on our own kind and on the other species with whom we share our planet.
When he received an honorary doctorate from the University of Victoria
in 2013, he wrote for his convocation address "an open letter to all the wild
creatures of the earth." It went viral on YouTube where you can still find it.

Six years later, as he lay dying, he ached not for himself but for the loss
of caribou and whales and owls and salmon. He bemoaned the clearcuts
and the forests burning in his home province. "I don't understand," he'd
say, "why all the commentaries focus on the destruction to property,
the human losses. No one mentions the animals and trees caught in the
fires." Each thought of a great cedar turning to ash, a bird exploding in the
branches, a bear or cougar unable to outrun the flames, entered his body
like a cinder and burned there.

Throughout his life he couldn't ignore that burning or the other fires
smoldering inside him, those ignited by poverty, injustice, violence and
shame. They drove him to his passion, his many decades of writing and
his generous encouragement of the hundreds of poetry pilgrims he guided
along the way. A poet who sang the darkness, he also found music for the

enlightened moment in the garden, the turtle in the mud, the cat presenting to his master the body of a mole. In wonder and wisdom, he found the notes and language of love and the deep quiet that he came to in himself.

His calling to poetry began when he was a young man working in the mill towns of British Columbia, and it never left him. About a month before he died, he gave me a folder of poems he'd been working on in the rare moments of grace he found in the midst of an enervating illness. "Take a look," he said. "I think I have a small book here." I thought so, too, and as we always did for one another, I made a few editing notes on the pages. He never felt well enough to return to these poems, and though most of my comments consisted of one word, "Wonderful," it fell to me after his death to pull the manuscript together and make the final cuts and edits. It was a daunting task because in our decades together, although we'd offered one another line-by-line advice, we did so delicately and knew when to back off and leave the decision up to the writer. I couldn't be delicate now. As I struck out an adjective or a line, sometimes a whole poem, I apologized out loud to Patrick. I said things like, "I hope you're okay with this." I turned the editing into a conversation, the final dialogue about poetry we would have, his voice in the poems stretching across the months of his absence, the rhythms he heard in his breath and blood entering my body as I sat at my computer with the stark beauty he created in the last few years of his life.

These fiercely alive words and the shadows they cast across the page were an amazing gift Patrick gave me. It is a gift he passes on to those who revere and read his poetry, including the students he worked with and adored. *The Quiet in Me* is in some ways a sweet and lyrical goodbye. It draws to an end the life work of one of our country's finest writers.

LIVING IN A PHANTOM HUT

A wolf-hair brush in a yellow jar, a pool at dawn,
Bashō on the road to the deep north.
There is nothing you can see that is not a flower;
there is nothing you can think that is not the moon.
A tuft of hair hooked on a strand of barbed wire,
a rusted fence above the Barrière River, white water,
old volcanoes, a crow picking at caribou bones, content.
Those mountains I wandered through when I was young.
There was a need for a small fire in the night. Still,
I wept back then for what could not be undone.
Old misfortunes can bring an old man peace.
My face reveals my face, my hands my hands.
There is nowhere I can go where I haven't been.
When I hold the brush to my ear I hear the moon.

HUMMINGBIRDS

They say you can pluck them like jewels
from the branches at night,
if you can find them sleeping
inside the shivering bamboo.
How many nights have I tried and failed,
full moon and crescent, the dark and the light?
I have searched in the black bamboo and the gold,
but who can find such a small heart?

BITTER

It is the honey lands you will leave,
the land of the bees and the fat birds calling.
It is the ash and grit of the fires you want
if only to weep over the memory of dry springs,
the long dreams that are the skulls of horses,
the empty marrow bones with their strings of red ants.
Surely you remember coarse salt on your tongue.
Come to me from beyond the fields and streams,
the sweet lands, the places of fruit and blossom,
the song of the falling water and wild birds.
Let your heart be the sound of the wind seething.
Sift with me the withered seeds in your fists.
Lie awake among stones in the creek beds.
Listen to the wind in the discarded flutes of the bones.

THE BREATH

A spring spider hangs from my finger.
I hold my breath, lay the line of silk across an apple branch.
The web she weaves will cover the whole world.

CHUCK BERRY AND CHERRY BLOSSOMS

The guide at the museum tells me there is no one here
who can read the script on the surimono, the poem
among the blossoms silent now. The radio is playing
Chuck Berry singing "Maybellene," and listening,
the song as out of place as I am, I no longer know
why I can't be true to what's still in me, my body
a museum for what's gone. The paper, centuries old,
is a whisper in the guide's frail hands.
I think no one will look at it again now that I am done.
Each hidden word is a fragile blossom, begging
why can't you be true, Chuck Berry's notes
drifting among the low boughs of the cherry trees,
the faraway sound of a V8 Ford chasing a Cadillac
and someone doing *the things you used to do.*

* A surimono is a Japanese wood-block print, created for circulation among friends,
  that combines words with delicate painted images.

A CHRISTMAS POEM

You get asked for a Christmas poem
to read on the radio—a poem for a friend,
a guy you know, and it gets you
thinking about Christmas and wondering
why you've never written one,
a Christmas poem, you mean, something
about birth and death, something
about stables and animals, the soft smell
of cattle in winter, the bloom of steam
rising from their horns, and chickens,
surely there'd be chickens, roosting,
quiet, even the rooster though he'd have an eye
on the sun coming, that first light breaking
over the hills, and a birth, yes, a baby, sure,
and you wonder at that, remembering
the time you, only twenty, a first-aid man
in a mill town, delivered a baby up north,
that slipperiness, that shout the baby gave
when he took in the whole world with his breath,
that kind of miracle wasn't the first
thing in your mind like the birth
in the stable in the story
you were told when you were little
and which now you rarely think of
because you know it's only a story,
a myth really, something made up to keep
children happy, and anyway it's been
written a hundred thousand times,
all those sentimental poems about Christmas,
and you swore long ago

you'd never go that way, but still
there was a birth and there was a child
and even if the stable was a wishfulness
with its goats and pigs, its chickens
and its horses, the hay laid down
and a blanket hung to keep the cold away
because it gets cold that time of year
even in the Holy Land, and a woman, yes,
there had to be a mother who took
that child to her breast and fed it, and
a father too, a little afraid, a little unsure
of what to do, helpless like men are
at ordinary miracles, like you were
up north, that baby sliding out of the woman
and you holding it for a moment, the woman
saying so soft you almost didn't hear,
"Give him to me," and you did
and sat beside her, quiet, only watched
that small face pressed against her,
young as you were, and you were young then,
saying nothing, the blood on your hands
her blood, not his, a rust-red, drying
in the air and then looking at you
with something in her face you didn't understand,
not then, not now, her tears without crying,
and the quiet in her after such a birth,
so poor she wouldn't go out to a doctor
and chose you, and what this has to do
with Christmas, you don't know, but it does
somehow because of the look she gave you
and the child and the blood on your hands
and the night, and everything so quiet in that room,
and you give these words to your friend,

not knowing if what you've written is enough
or whether it's even about Christmas,
but it's as close as you can get to it, her look
and the baby lying there, quiet, and the years.

COBALT BLUE

The elephant seals in the Bay of Otters.
I sat under the arbutus at dawn and watched the calves at play.
Gulls screamed as geese lifted on their cowled wings.
There were clicks of beetles on the tree's bronze flesh.
One grandfather raised his trunk, the holes where his tusks were, healed.
Two eagles in their mating swung the sky together, talons locked in their gyre.
The light from their bodies, glancing, took me back to Chartres,
the ancient windows of the cathedral, that blue glass.
The mind is without time. *Le bleu de l'aube.*
No one has been able to make that colour again.

THE ELDER TREE

Today I cleared the earth around the elder tree,
moved the dead branches the wind had carried
to where I come to pray. And today the turtle rose
from the pond's heavy dark to heal her winter shell.
She rises in the spring when the light returns.
I leaned against the ancient bark, closed my eyes and saw
my father planting trees, his hands caring for the roots.
How long ago the fathers, their stories another kind of cure.
The sun mends most wounds, each prayer I say beneath the tree
the oldest prayer. Her branches in the wind sing to me:
I am the tree who rests on the back of the turtle the turtle rests upon.

THUMBPRINT

Qin Shi Huang walled the potters inside
his perfect city of death. Their hands remain
in the curved cheekbones of the warriors.
Inside the eye socket of the last horse,
the thumbprint of its maker.
The eye stares sightless upon the potter
who stares sightless in return.

* Qin Shi Huang was the emperor responsible for the making and burial of the
terracotta army to guard his tomb.

CAREFULLY

The mole in his small room
moves a small stone
and waits out the rain.

ELLINGTON & VERA LYNN

I was a boy singing out from the wrong town
in the wrong country, "The White Cliffs of Dover,"
the soldiers marching down to the ships in Nanaimo.
Sometimes we are again small children, only just.
There was a girl I knew whose father hurt her.
She walked down the midnight street in Salmon Arm,
small, naked, her outstretched arms like wings.
She rode the wind into no one's story.
Who remembers her now? She asked my mother
for a bit of bread, the stump of a loaf
my mother gave her, and turned then away.
There are nights we fall asleep to the songs of dead angels.
I sang to my father in Kent at my mother's bidding.
The wives around the kitchen table said, *Again, again.*
Sing him home, my mother whispered.
He couldn't hear me from that mountain room, the ships leaving.
Years later he came back, the guns of the Normandy beaches in his head.
O love, are you my mother on her death bed saying she hated
the song she made me sing? "Mood Indigo" was hers
despite the bluebirds high above the cliffs.

SMALL ELEGY

The silence of the dead is what we own.
It's why we sing. The sky is clear today.
Go on, I hear my father say, my mother too,
and though they rest in sunken graves
I hear them still. The sky is clear today,
the harvest weeks away and no forests burn.
The dead sing in the rubble and the fires.
We must listen to their song.
Their burden is our lives.
We pray because we cannot turn away.

ENKIDU, WAITING

The carp places a single bubble under the ice.
Her body eats her now, the feathers of her gills pale.
In the night of the March full moon, the ice will open,
and her winter song will rise to me, breaking
from the deep world. Welcome, Shamhat.
Spring and thin salvation.

---

* In the ancient epic *Gilgamesh,* the gods form a human out of clay and call him
  Enkidu. He grows up in the woods living as a wild man with the animals until he is
  seduced by a beautiful woman, Shamhat. She entices him to leave the wilderness
  and adopt the ways of the civilized world.

FALSE CREEK

She walked away into the rain and became the rain,
her land buried in false rainbows, oil slick on the waters
pumped from the bilges of the tugs as they dragged
the ancient forests to where the saws spun screaming.
I remember her hands, the callus lines she wore
from making baskets, the weave so tight they could carry water,
and her laughter. Even I, who was young and rough
and didn't know much, knew the beauty of her making,
the woman who became the rain.

FOG ON THE SOUTH SHORE

Even the gulls
        have lost their way.

ICEBERGS OFF FOGO ISLAND

It is the quiet we love, the way water touches us,
the iceberg an animal gone astray in search of time.
The water that is ice is ten thousand years old.
The sea slides across its shine, caresses
the frozen curves, the arabesques of blue and green
and white. The rocks off Joe Batt's Arm
speak silently of snow, the wind that wears them away.
Each wave brings water back to water.
As if the iceberg is a child come home,
and, found at last, melts into the arms of its mother.

KINTSUGI

The raccoon washes with slender fingers a broken moon.
Fog forms dew on my face and I weep without intent.
Over the waters the crippled cedars hang in the remains of storms.
Their branches reach now for the sea.
Like the raccoon, I'm distracted by the task at hand.
As now, the scars without my body greater than the scars within.
Bones shine through my skin.
Tonight I cradled my woman as she slept the night. Such peace.
I am outside myself, without disguise.
There is only a little left to know. Water returns to water.
The dew in my eyes, a moment ago an ocean.
On the face of the golden puddle the moon repairs itself again, and yet again.

---

* Kintsugi, "golden repair," is the Japanese art of repairing broken pottery by mixing
lacquer with powdered gold. The repair of a broken bowl is only one of its many
possible beauties.

LITTLE WOLF

Even the wolf spider hides from me who would save it.
The ice melts, a liquid ribbon by the sprung door.
At Little Hell's Gate the Overlanders watched the river
break their rafts to pieces, a single blanket,
white with three Hudson Bay bars, a soggy floating island
somehow saved three miles south below Poplar Flats.
And written down so we would remember their joy. So,
I walk the hall each night in search of what's been lost,
come down to pleading with a wolf spider for its life.
How mad am I? At the elder tree I took my face
in my cupped hands and offered it to the wind.
My poor mouth could taste the salt from the bay. In God's name
how did I live those years in the canyon a century after
their struggle? I remember bowing to a chocolate lily on a scree,
wishing its life free of our desire to ruin such beauty, the Overlander
women wailing, cups and saucers broken, the little they had of the past,
the blue fragment of English china I found in gravel
below the Gate where the waters break at last.
And who will break me now that I am broken?
Little wolf who weaves no web, who hides from me,
come to my hand that I might be made free.

* The Overlanders, a group of around 150 settlers, traveled from Fort Garry,
  Manitoba, to the Cariboo gold fields of British Columbia in the 1800s. Little Hell's
  Gate is the name given to the narrowing of the canyon through which the North
  Thompson River flows.

BLUEBERRY HILL

She had collected his books of poems for years,
saving him in boxes and on the long dry shelves
on the wall away from the blinds. She was the wife
of his friend who was in the living room, drunk,
listening to Fats Waller, the early records
Waller made when he was young, the music
old with that hiss grooves learn
after too many plays. She'd taken him
to her room to show him the collection,
the books he'd written years ago
when he didn't know there was something
besides himself, something other than the *I*
he thought he was, standing there thinking,
her on her knees, taking him
into her mouth, looking up to make sure
he was watching, and his friend
calling to them from the living room, saying
they needed to hear this, the best cut,
Listen to this, he said.

LACRIMAE

Each day another kind of dark and I begin
where colour slips away. My eyes find nothing.
Surely the old gods meant it so,
shadows in my hands, the way they play upon me
in the night, music from my mother's tomb.
What wonder it was to swim inside her,
hear her drum song beating. In that womb was
another kind of calling, the one eelgrass knows
in the narrows where herring lay their eggs.
To see through a whole body, the new life
small as a stickleback at play
among the bright waves, the creature I was
when she created in her sea my heart.

LOVE, TOO

And the flowers, her wet scent, lupines,
their seeds a thousand years old blooming after snow,
and sweet arnica, saxifrage, and anemones, her hair tumbling.
Yes, and the creek rising from the rocks, the glacier in retreat.
And the ptarmigan too, changed, the white fading as the last snow.
You dunk your mouth in water and drink the mountain
in your dark becoming. A broken sky and want, light almost gone,
the meteors born out of what blood, falling upon your eyes; the woman
who rises in the dark, her hair tumbling, and does not return.

MORNING

(for Lorna)

Leaf is leaf, stone is stone, sand the beginning,
the end of hills, the land worn away to ripples by the wind.
The grasses whisper, seed to flower to seed, a moth
asleep on her wrist in the dawn, in this remote present, this now.

Earth is the awakening, stem and root, between them breath,
ankle and foot, breast and belly, the unfolding that is a woman,
the scent of her rising, her yes to morning, the story that is night,
a child hiding in the caragana bushes, a mother calling her home.

Her bear has been saved on the estuary, the wolf in the clear-cut,
the blossom, the bee. In her hands are many hands, paw and fin,
wing and wonder. Her blood flows with the hearts of the many,
the risen in her clenched fists, the fallen in her open palms.

THE MOSQUE OF THE DROP OF BLOOD

Shadows in the market rubble grieve the soles of empty shoes,
the unbound hair, the teeth golden in the sun.
It takes all the darkness in the world to make bones shine.
Bats flutter through rib cages, the homes of all our hearts.
There are no metaphors, no misfortune greater than
a woman at the well of empty skulls. No rope
can reach the stars in the minarets of old Aleppo
or those that stud the sky inside an empty womb.
Surely we are all undone by a single drop of blood.

MOVING, DAY

My father still, dead, at last, and the young bumblebee,
one of the slaves sent out for nectar, her trembling
as I caress her back in the bowl of the rose, and too,
on my knees after, this odd prayer that my father be forgotten,
as all things are and will be, the whisper of her wings.
Heavy with pollen she weaves through the tumbled blooms,
as I kneel in the morning, having come at last to my home.

ÖTZI

Wanting to be lost as he was when he was young, farther back,
deep into the mountains, the creek without a name taking him away
so that he did not know whose hands, whose face was in the quiet pool
where the grizzlies drank, their ancient paw prints deep in the earth.
I have let go of what I am, he said, and smiled, the old master
alive in him still. And perhaps he was right, hope an illusion too,
and rose then into the evening, refusing direction, finally knowing
where he wasn't. The grizzly road followed the water, the creek
narrow, and he knew he was close to the spring, high in the yellow cedar
below the alpine where the last meadows began, above them sere rock,
the crevices where the snow waited, and he walking without fear into the last ice.

---

* Ötzi was the Iceman of the fourth millennium BC whose desiccated body was
found high in the Ötztal Alps of Italy in 1991.

PERIPHERY

The moon caught in the sky where the cave opened,
his body far inside, the nest a grey lamp,
a frenzy of wasps flying in, the glare behind him
turned and dark, fractured into dust and fragile webs. Their wings,
their thin-wired whine, their black legs slung under as they flew
before him into the cave, the moon hooked on the mouth,
and the wasps as they greeted him, slender bodies
hanging from his hair, the bare flesh of his arms,
the scratch of infinitesimal thorns on his chest and hands,
and how he breathed their sharp metallic reek,
their song what he was and was to be,
the swollen blooms that were the wounds they left him
that his mother knew when she touched him in the kitchen,
the Wild Rose stove huge and burning, her cold hands on his skin,
in her eyes a sorrow that wasn't when she turned away.

POVERTY SUTRA

Desert pine, the wind a pale needle in drought
that numbs the heart. In the dust a white soul returning.
The dead crowd in, the old ones with their broken shoes.
Dry poppy bells ring their changes. They lead me to the place
where cicadas cut stone into silence.
I lost the mind I had when I was young. Half-blind
these eyes have a desert in them. I walk the arroyo,
my words spare as the seeds of poverty grass
that fall on wasted ground.

There is a quiet in me: the old man I lifted today from the pavement, his
    weight beyond being,
his legs useless, his wheelchair a step away, and he was like some warrior fallen
from his horse, his tank, his life. Staggering I danced with him, his muscled
    arms in mine,
his legs moving like the empty wings of a bird just dead. And I was suddenly
back there in that cabin in the north, lifting a body to a bed, and dead,
    and dead
the weight of him, an old man, all parchment skin and rickets, all what?
    The body newly dead
falls, limber as tired rubber, heavy as the world. How long ago now since I
    laid the old
prospector, my friend, on his cot and covered him, not out of shame, but as
    I might have covered
a woman sleeping after love? And so too this fallen man I lifted
    from the parking lot,
his wife wringing her hands, the sound of her skin whispering, and
    thank you, thank you,
she said, the man grinning up at me from his chair as he settled his legs,
    and done,
wheeled himself away, leaving me with his muscles still in my hands, and
    too, the other
man, my friend, dead now these many years, who fought in the Boer War
    and who rode the rails
with the unemployed and homeless to Regina, having washed his flesh
    clean of poverty,
having dressed him and covered him with earth, the lovers too I laid to rest
in the sleep that follows love, all the arms I've held, such arms as will hold me.

ROAD CREW, AUGUST, 1956

Bluegrass and brome and the tufted hair grass on the verge
where the gravel breaks, splotches of tar still soft, the huge machine
stopped, the cry of the sprayer stilled, ten miles to Riske Creek.
And the minuscule insect eggs, the mites, the impossibly small,
the living smothered, the roof of a Western meadowlark's nest
split by a passing foot, the thatch torn away, and the eggs
the hesitant female turns with her beak, wet with tar, and the road crew
lounging in the machine's shade, one young man, his lank penis in his hand,
pissing by the ditch where the grasses lie flattened and black,
a stag beetle crawling from beneath dry chips, and the man
aiming at it, the sun above, and the sky, and the dust stretching into oblivion.

IT'S FINALLY FRIDAY

Nothing's better than pushing 12×2×20-foot fir into a CN boxcar going to
    Baton Rouge.
Christ, I was young then, a hundred pounds of green fir a feather
    in my hands.
The plank surged over the steel roller, through the sunburst air, and into
    the car.
There's no word I write can make that sound when it belled against
    the car's steel wall.
Wood ripped from the heart, over and over, my hands lifting dead weight,
    my rough hands
beating time, Jimmy Deloup singing "It's Friday Finally," quarter to five
    and counting.
"Dance Figure" is running through my head, Old Ezra telling me
    both of us are right.
Jimmy's in the car catching, working the restack, building our FVC boxcar
    for Louisiana,
the beer at Chilly Creek whispering our names. It's a quarter to freedom,
    Jimmy's
sister in the pickup truck, and I'm waiting for her grin. She's down from
    the Monashee,
none like thee among the dancers, dark eyes watching me and she's close
    to smiling.

SALT BURNER

Back then I stood at an iron sink after hours on the green chain,
scraped sap from my hands with steel wool.
The salt I burned was for a child crying in a ditch.
Her father stared past her from a logging truck, crazed
as he tried to make the cut block to catch a last load.
Poverty is meat wasting on the bones, a mother's eyes
dry as tinder burning in the dark. Tell those who ask
I know of salt, how it leaches from our flesh in terrible fires.

SALVATION

Listen to the prayers the leaves make
before they fall. So many dragonflies
shattering their wings in the night.
The sun fled so slowly I forgot it was gone.
Surely the time of the white breathing
is upon us, snow finding its way
into the sere valleys of the south.
I listen and know we are the naked ones,
our skin remembering the savannah
as we watch the early moon. The sound
of the leaves as they pull away from the tight buds
is our one salvation.

SLICK

My father laid his blade, *slick… slick… slick,*
upon my arm, the fine hair falling, whispers in the oil.
Steel dust glittered on my skin, my arm a sky at night.
I understand what he taught me only now:
a blade is a sigh, a trout caught in the mountains,
the flight of willow leaves. They move in the wind without number.
How hard it is to remember I forget, to forget I remember.
My scar is only one of my father's teachings.
Listen: the trout remains in shadow as the creek passes by.
The fallen leaf gets to shore by walking on water.

THE SEA IS OUR HOME

Each house turns its back to the sea,
no stairs built to climb to the front door.
Each window is a widow's walk,
each boat a man come home to rest.

SNOW

Snow falls in the night, little ghosts, little whispers.
The song of the pine needles is the sky resting on glass.
Painted turtles under the ice recall their last gulp of air
before they buried their bodies deep in the mud as the dark
devoured the sun. We dance without end in forgotten footprints,
a people walking as they left their land forever.
A stone found on Machu Picchu remembers the shadow of a condor,
a drop of rain on Angkor Wat, the fall of fretted ice on pin-tk-tn.
Do not say we are without a path, the way of the grease trails remains.
We gather from the sky little ghosts, little whispers among the stars.

* In the tongue of the indigenous Syilx people, "pin-tk-tn" was the place near their home (modern Penticton) where they believed the Okanagan River would flow forever.

SUICIDE

Salt on his tongue, tears, maybe, no, not crying, yet.
False Creek and lying, foolish, on his back as at the lake
when he floated out, the sun huge, bloated, and the coyote on the shore
watching. Even then, a boy, sinking, knew no mercy.
Now the Burrard Bridge, black water, headlights, swift quick moths,
night shouts and laughter, and his body a skin spear,
a bone arrow flying down, melting into the sea.
Cold and salt, a roar above him. And now risen,
his head floated in the swill, his body where?
Someone's legs moving below him, slow scissors thick with water.
And the high windows, one light, a woman still there.
The Cecil Hotel, her dancing, impaled upon a metal pole.
Bright moths breathing, quick under the bridge, his arms
around a piling, cold tar, and how, clothes unfolded and
shaken, he dressed, walked barefoot back to the bar, his boots stolen.

THIS WAY

The whisper of the turtle in the sun, her gasp as of love breaking.
And no other, a shadow fleeting, a merlin passing through without striking.
What beauty in this remnant signature, and I rise to that, mortal, without fear.
As I bow down, the capsules of the moss open around me.
So too the bamboo, who learned to bend before the wind.
I bend to the living dust, quiet beside my teacher.
My elder tree spoke once to a forest farther than the mind.
Within her roots lies a cave where river otters come to rest.
In the reek of forgotten kills is the bed where I lie down.

WILD DOGS, 1959

Wild dogs in the high country, hunting them, on horses, a roan mare
under Johnny Singletrout and me following in the pickup truck.
Finding my way through sagebrush and stunted rose.
Early morning gone, three calves run to death, and a steer barely alive,
head bowed as to a priest, how his breath left him in a single heave,
legs splayed and down. And Johnny turned away, wrist to his eye.
A Shepherd cross, three years from lame, and running hard to die,
in the bunchgrass, whimpers, shy and begging, his black tongue
wet with wrong blood, and behind him, two feral bitches hiding in the pines.
And the chopping block after, where I wield steel, knee deep
in split wood, winter far enough away and close enough
to worry, the year mostly gone, a cut moon on the crest of the Cascades.

WITHOUT ART AND WAITING

He struggled with the moss on the rock, trying to find the way.
Lost, the creek he followed emptied into a land-locked lake.

There are guardians everywhere, the migrant birds
melting as the moon rises. Feathered messengers fleeing the night.

How many years will it take to forget the disasters, the droughts,
the floods that took them out to sea singing songs to confuse the sailors.

The man uncovered in the alley, lights shining down
on his lost face. Mighty nations, besieged cities.

The forms shame takes, the way it withers the body. It cringes,
indecent, a book without covers, every page smudged, erased.

I found you in the Street of Storms where the iceman cried his trade.
There was something mortal in our love-making, unseen, unheard.

This much is known, words recited in the dark, innumerable birds,
mice scurrying in their tunnels of woven grass, little bronze bells.

ASH

(for Sean Virgo)

A lone goose flying through the alders
is only a lone goose. My friend holds his daughter in a jar.
There was a moment on a porch years ago,
pulling on his boots up on the islands, but why
he remembers this is not a question he can ask.
Leather strands loop around his fingers.
He pulls the laces tight, a steady rain falling
on the Haida Gwaii of late December. The body weighs
almost nothing when the bones are crushed, the flesh
flown into some outer dark, the smoke for a moment
obscuring the sun. He'll leave some ashes on the islands,
the rest in Scotland. It's what she wants.
If he waits forever a goose will appear as it did
the day he stepped out into the rain. Back then
he left a box of dry fir and kindling by the stove
as if his daughter would come back.
The cry of a barnacle goose circled above him.
He knows everything now and nothing.
The fire across the river burns itself slowly out.

OM

How thin the night, a mole's cry waking me. In dream
my ear was to the dark, an earthworm in its tunnel waiting.
I feel my brittle bones and smile. I am as fragile as winter grass.
I think of leaping to the floor and don't.
Like my old cat I climb down slowly, accept
the smile of my woman who gives me coffee in the morning.
She makes me want to remember when we moved
naked in a summer far away.
How sweet our laughter on the grey stones touching…
and so the prince set out on the road to discover suffering
and gave his self up at the last. Ah, thinking won't get me there either.
My work is always close at hand. The cat purrs and offers me his prey.
A headless mole, his fur the colour of the moon.

* The prince is Siddhartha who became the Buddha.

LOOKOUT

Sometimes we look out over the great plains
and see a faint light falling between what we think are mountains.
It is then we know we are living far from the world.

As the abandoned hulk of a turtle you found in a field
miles from water. How you squatted on your bare heels and gazed
with the eyes of a child at the bulk of that green dome.

Or the night you stood by the redwood tree on the street outside your house
and stared through the burden of heavy needles at your wife
as she stared out of the light. How for one moment you were afraid.

Sometimes we live far from the world.
Without thought, and wanting.

HOW MANY TIMES HAVE I TAKEN OUT MY DEATH?

Was there ever time to see the stars
above the stink of False Creek mouth
where I drowned myself over and over,
my body slipping like a born lamb into the blood
that is the salt water of this other, older birth,
my mouth opening to drag the sea in,
the risen fish breaking into air?
Death, you sullen master, come
find me in the waters of my birth. Don't let me
live so long that I must call you friend, following
you as a dog does, servile, whining.

FRAGMENTS

Shards and splinters I paw through, woodshed litter,
bits of bark and dust, fragments of fir and hemlock I see
and cannot touch, the mind grasping at chips and flakes,
a chopping block, stiff feathers stuck in blood,
a head that sees through a grey slit all that is and was,
a yellow beak split so the tongue still tastes the air,
an axe buried in the round fir, the shaft worn smooth
by heavy hands, and in the broken wall the sun sliding
as if already dead, the light burying itself in a square
upon the floor where a barefoot child lights a fold of paper
and singes the faint feather hairs on a bird's legs and breast,
and yes, I would reach out and touch the boy, my hand
upon his thin shoulder and tell him ... tell him what?
That seventy-three years will come to add to his seven,
and in the waste and trash of hours there will be
every tangled dream and desolation, all human wants
and wishes, blood and bone, small deaths and large,
each birth, each son, a daughter, wives, and women,
every bleak defeat and loss, the resurrections, visions,
and more, and less, and a man who wishing, wishes
well this child who holds in his hands an open flame.

ACKNOWLEDGEMENTS

Thank you to the wonderful folks at Harbour, including Marisa Alps, Anna Comfort O'Keeffe, Coralie Worsley and the publisher extraordinaire, Howard White. And kudos to Elaine Park, for her sharp copy-editing eye. All were such a pleasure to work with in a difficult time. Thank you, as well, to Micheline Maylor of *Freefall* for publishing a special edition dedicated to Patrick Lane and to Barry Callaghan of *Exile* for featuring several of Patrick's new poems and submitting them for the National Magazine Awards, where they won the 2010 Gold Medal for poetry.

—Lorna Crozier, January 2022

Photo credit: Gary McKinstry

ABOUT THE AUTHOR

Patrick Lane, considered by most writers and critics to be one of Canada's finest poets, was born in 1939 in Nelson, BC. He grew up in the Kootenay and Okanagan regions of the BC Interior, primarily in Vernon. He came to Vancouver and co-founded a small press, Very Stone House, with bill bissett and Seymour Mayne. He then drifted extensively throughout North and South America. He worked at a variety of jobs, from labourer to industrial accountant, but much of his life was spent as a poet. He was also the father of five children and grandfather of nine. He won nearly every literary prize in Canada, from the Governor General's Literary Award to the Canadian Authors Association Award to the Dorothy Livesay Prize. In 2014, he became an Officer of the Order of Canada, an honour that recognizes a lifetime of achievement and merit of a high degree. In 2019 for his life work in poetry, he was awarded the prestigious, international Homer Prize, The European Medal of Poetry and Art. His poetry and fiction have been widely anthologized and translated into many languages. His more recent books include *Witness: Selected Poems 1962–2010* (Harbour Publishing, 2010), *The Collected Poems of Patrick Lane* (Harbour Publishing, 2011), *Washita* (Harbour Publishing, 2014; shortlisted for the 2015 Governor General's Literary Award), *Deep River Night* (McClelland & Stewart, 2018) and a posthumous collection, *The Quiet in Me* (2022). Lane spent the later part of his life in Victoria, BC, with his wife, the poet Lorna Crozier. He died in 2019.